The Year I Learned to Fly

A mystical, magical, and wildly imaginative
devotional

Rachael Cannon

Dedication

To the One whose arms
are holding me now,
Never a doubt,
I am yours.

To my family,
I am certain
of the bonds
of our love.

For Mandy,
My sister
And my best friend.

Preface

With great delight, I share these personal glimpses of my aerial adventures with you.

I have found the immutable love of God in mysterious, magical, and imaginative little places that have changed my life.

I wish that as you read, your wings will begin to flutter, and you take to the sky.

Once you have ridden the wind, it isn't exciting to write about earthbound things.

The sky is my home. It's the loving lap of my Father in his heavenly throne room. I've been placed here by nail-scarred hands holding me now, even as I write. I've sat here under his wing, feeling his warmth, hearing his heartbeat, and listening to him tell me his endless whispers of love until my wings began to flutter. I'm learning to live from his opinion of me.

I hope you sense his nearness and enjoy your ascent. Fly carefree and unfettered by anything earthly, and most of all, live loved.

1

Without Flaw Within

He plants the seedlings. The sprouts are growing into strong stems, the branches are budding, and the buds are blossoming beautifully.

Did she begin in her mother's womb or when she was a spark in her Father's eyes, before time? Or did she begin when she awakened to love's wonder?

Anyway, she is happening.

She is changing, blossoming.

Love is reminiscing of Oneness, in the beginning, before, before.

Love is changing how she thinks and believes about him, her, and others.

He watches her grow. She grows in the dark and the light, in the day and the night. She grows when she cries, and she grows when she laughs.

And he says,
Oh, she's perfect.
She couldn't be any more perfect.
I have made a sign and wonder, and she is growing and
transforming beautifully.

He sums her whole life up in his words,
Without flaw within.

He whispers to her heart,
I'm so excited about your life, darling.

2

Fly

I'm on the edge of a new life that has always been mine. The life he designed for me to live.

It's only scary at the beginning, the butterflies whisper.

Who told you you were not like me?
Who told you you were naked?
Who told you you were just a girl?
Who told you you could not fly?

Why would I be afraid unless what he sees and what I see are two different realities? Love is opening my eyes to see what he knows to be true about me. I am beginning to think like my Father.

> *Come to the edge, he said.*
> *We can't; We're afraid, they responded.*
> *Come to the edge, he said.*
> *We can't; We'll fall, they responded.*
> *And so they came.*
> *And he pushed them.*
> *And they flew.*
> *Christopher Logue*

3

Sun Rise

She learned to trust during the night that seemed to last forever.

The darkest night will end. The sun will rise, and a new day will dawn.

Somewhere beyond the darkness, dawn was breaking, surpassing the bitter night.

A morning glory grows in the darkness. Even dark waters have a snowy white foam.

She has been through dark times. She can hear them in other people's voices and see them in their eyes. She reminds herself of love's hovering presence in the darkness and expects the sweet song of light.

She is not afraid of the dark. She knows that darkness is only an announcement of impending light.

She is certain of the sunrise. The sun has never not risen for her.

4

Exploring Raindrops

She is an explorer. One time she forgot to explore and almost died.

She learned that being who you are is as essential as breathing.

In breathing, we discover our likeness and which aspects of his nature we embody most.

Just as raindrops are in the ocean and the ocean in the raindrops, nothing can separate them.

She searches the rain and discovers a Man-Lamb alive in the inmost ocean of her heart. She spends her time bonding with him.

She is determined to explore as much of his love, nature, world, eyes, hands, and heart as she can in her lifetime (wink).

She ventures into the unexplored regions of the rain and writes an account of her voyages.

5

Raison d'etre

The French have a wonderful phrase that rolls off the tongue, *raison d'etre*.

Its meaning is the most important reason or purpose for someone or something's existence.

She is his *raison d'etre*, his reason for being. She is why he became human.

I loved thee first, he whispers to her heart.

He has set his affection on her and is determined to rescue her from a distorted relationship.

His very existence, his *raison d'etre*, is for his darlings to live in union with him.

They are inseparable. The two have become one. The thrill of living in his arms never diminishes. She cannot exist without him, nor he without her.

She is the reason he exists, and now he is hers.

6

The Land Under

I explore the kingdom of life. It's an endless adventure, plunging the depths of his love and grace and the rising peaks of his mercy.

Everything is alive inside this realm of life and communicates in sounds, smells, waves, hums, hues, and sensations.

It is as if all living things cannot contain enough compliments for his handiwork. Therefore, the creation cannot stop exalting the Creator because they see him in all of life.

Blades of grass shiver as I pass by in the sheer wonder of his beauty made tangible in me.

The lilies say, *Good Day, felicitous One.*
I say, *Hello, my boujee friends.*

Love flows through the land; everyone is kind, and I go about exploring the land under his Lordship.

Drink the Rain

One time it rained in reverse. The secret spring hidden in the fountains of the deep boiled over and burst up from the earth.

I was sitting in my room, in his breath, beholding him. Then, up from the floor, water droplets began to rain from the deep.

Time stood still, and the droplets suspended in midair.

I held them in my fingers and tasted one. It tasted like honey and new dirt. I marveled how love could easily elude the laws of gravity to make me smile.

There were letters and pictograms I'd never seen in the raindrops, and they rained in my mouth and on my skin.

Drink the rain, my heart whispered.

Suddenly, what seemed like an ancient language made perfect sense to me.

Grapson! Now write!

Can a book become a Man?
Can a Man become a book?
If raindrops were words,
I would drink them
and become a living word.

Photini

Photini, the light woman, walks around and emits light. Even her smile seems to catch the light.

She converts light to energy. She is photosynthesizing.

Don't be flimsy, she says.
All I had was the look in his eyes
That's all it took.
Don't rely on a book or a passage
When you can live in his look.
You can't argue with his eyes.

Hooked on a look, she became the light of the world. Living Water found her at the well and gave her eternal life, a secret spring was sprung.

She took a drink of the life that is light, and she still shines. She's still telling all who meet her of his great love.

She opened a doorway into everlasting life at the bottom of a dry well and fell into love's arms forever.

9

Eternal Hearts

He hid eternity in my heart, and I found it. When others went searching inside for separation, I saw him.

Eureka! I have discovered a Man of the purest heart inside me.

The Ever Unfolding One has made way for me to live agelessly enfolded in his incredible love.

I found the secret of *aionos zoe*, ages and ages of life, and I write of the poetry of life, of living face to face with Da Da. I was in him since the beginning.

I began in Da Da's eternal love bosom, in his most profound feelings of emotion and desire. I found eternal life by knowing him and sharing what he believes to be true about me.

I remember I'm born beneath the Son of another world, so I live from the eternal dimension.

10

The Alcove

One day she found an alcove hidden under his left arm, and she snuggled into his side. So hidden from the world, only he knows she's there. She spends hours there, telling him of her love for him. And he sings to her, and her body hums, and her veins turn from turquoise to white. She glows a little a first, translucent. It feels like a womb, safe and like a warm bath, and she feels nurtured. She begins to grow here like a newborn baby feeding on her mother.

She eats him and feels life in unimaginable ways. In this womb of wonder, she remembers he hid her in him before the world began.

She found a hidden door in the side of the alcove under his wing. There's blood over the door. She knocks on the door, and the door is delighted. *Come in*, she hears.

And she knows before she enters that nothing will ever be the same again, and she crosses the threshold. She lets go of earthly things that define her and enters the One.

11

Greater Reality

She is becoming acquainted with greater realities. Finally, she's found her place in the Father's love lap.

She lives in two worlds. She has one foot in one world and one foot in the other.

She lives in the kingdom of the Son, ruled by the love of all loves. Love Rules. She sits on a throne of love. He took the judgment for all of mankind. He erased the sin of the whole world; he can't remember it. That's love.

The unseen eternal realm within her has her full attention and captivates her gaze.

She occupies her mind with greater realities. Nothing earthly; only the love of Christ defines her life.

Flush your thoughts with truth.

The kingdom within you is greater than the kingdom of this world.

12

The Covert Family

She has a secret family of angels and saints.
They are for her, cheering her on, preserving
her life, protecting her, providing for her daily
needs, and more. They covertly guide her into
mysteries of deep and long-lost treasures. They
are her hidden allies and a secret source of
encouragement.

When she explores roads less traveled, they are
there to encourage her along the way.

Sometimes they look like small clouds, a mist or
puff of smoke in the air in front of her; other
times, she sees them as flashes of light or senses
their nearness, guiding her.

They've lifted their earth anchors and set sail on
the Golden Sea, but sometimes take a shore
leave to come back and share things they have
seen or heard of him.

They travel the earth on the ebbs and currents
of love.

13

Freedom

Freedom is essential to her.

She wasn't born to spend time in a cage, look like other people, or believe like others. So she broke out of the box.

She was born again to be free and live wide open. Life runs rampant through her veins, and it's vibrant in every way. It is life within her life.

She is freeborn, Sarah's daughter, begotten in love from above. She's as free as the wind and has that twinkle in her eye. She knows something we don't know, and she isn't afraid.

Free and unfettered, careless in the care of her Father. She has her eye on the One no eye has seen, and she keeps right on living, flying.

All the outcomes were necessary to bring her into this wide, open space of luscious greenness.

Her freedom is contagious.

14

Singing Sands

She goes to the shoreline every day in search of him. She always finds him in one way or another.

Walk with Me, Little Lamb (the name he gave her). *Lose yourself in Me. Let's blur the lines of where you begin and end.*

They walked hand in hand, her Beloved and his Betrothed, although you couldn't tell the difference between them.

They spoke to each other in sounds, looks, nearness, or thoughts, and their meaning so deep it thundered through her.

She could feel herself trembling as his thoughts released waves of love energy that rippled through her and into the sand.

My well-pleased opinion of you is the only thing that matters, and she could hear his heart as if it were in her chest.

I am well-pleased with you. The sand trembled and rippled and whistled at his voice.

Booming dunes began singing the song of the sands, each grain responding to his voice as if they had heard it before. She remembered R. A. Bangnold and smiled.

His voice drifted from his heart to hers, and the sands rippled and sang the song of sons.

As the sands trembled at his voice, the waves broke, kissing his feet sweetly. Then as if the water remembered, it touched him and rushed to him. She gasped as she saw the little broken wave absorb him and run up his legs to his heart. He threw his head back and roared in laughter as if it tickled.

Yes, my creation, return to Me and remember our Oneness. I have come to release the world of its decay and restore life in every way imaginable.

Then the waters rushed back to the sea, knowing and glowing with translucent emerald color. Each wave was rising and falling at his greatness. When she looked at him again, he wore an emerald glowing halo.

She felt a drop of water on her face and wiped it off. The droplet smiled at her before jumping back into the sea.

She hears the whisper of the waves, and they call him *Yeshua, the Wonder Child.*

The golden sand showed his footprints and whispered a little under his step.

He is the *Sand Reckoner, the Locorum Supputator.* He tells her about the grains of the sand, and he calls each one by name.

And she loves him even more than she did a second ago.

15

The Shallows

Leave the shallows of your old mind and venture with Me into the deep ocean of My endless love. Plunge into the depths of the extravagance of grace that forgets all association with muddled love songs.

Search and explore My goodness that knows no bounds. You are free. You are no longer held captive in a phony fortress of underrated thoughts about the Father or yourself. There are no undertows of shame or condemnation in the waves of his love. Instead, every second he pulls you deeper into his lovingkindness.

Feel the consciousness of grace.

Every thought that could trigger a malicious threat to your redeemed innocence drowns in the ocean of his love. So, rise above the dwarfed opinions about yourself.

Grasshoppers can't swim in milk and honey.

Swim past the shallows and dive deep. Listen to the melody of love from above.

16

Reflecting I Am

He leads me by still waters so I can see my reflection and remember who I AM. I see him in my face, and I remember the face of my birth. This remembering restores and reboots my soul to the beginning when I was face to face with him.

Even when my path winds through the dark marshes of tears, I dig deep to find a pleasant pool where others see only pain. I grow stronger and stronger with every step forward (Francois du Toit).

Goodness and mercy never let me get too far ahead. I will rest safe and easy for the rest of my life in my Father's hands.

He assured me that my body was a desirable home for him. My assurance comes from his protection and provision; he is the lord of his house. Therefore, he makes the necessary arraignments for me to be found safe and secure in his love.

My cup runs over and over and over.

17

Look Up

He has hidden his love everywhere, in everything, and in the least likely places waiting to be discovered, remembered, and experienced.

I've found hidden love treasures just by stopping to take a breath and look up in the middle of a busy day. With so many people looking down these days, you might find something special if you look up.

I'm discovering the lost art of looking.

Lift your eyes, darling. Trade your view for mine.

I look up and see what he's been looking at, and it's otherworldly.

Love's eyes see beyond the naked eye and into the unseen realm of the kingdom of the heart.

I am determined to find beauty and value in everything and everyone. I look for the heart in every place, thing, person, and situation.

18

Invisible Waterways

She can't remember where she met Phillipos, the horse-loving man, but they know each other. He rides horses and tides.

I want to show you something, he says. They wade into the water about waist deep, hugged by the waves. She felt the warm waves holding her like a power greater than her body. She felt herself being pulled into endless light, encapsulated by love.

Suddenly they are transported to another shore.

Later she learns the invisible river is a network of waterways, an entirely hidden and delightful way of transportation to places, worlds, dimensions, and realities.

The ocean of his endless love has a life hidden within the life seen on the surface. Timeless currents beneath what the eye sees and only the heart can follow.

So she rides the secret tide carrying the Good News to all who'll listen.

19

Point Clear

Welcome to Point Clear. I am giving you a new vista. Some call this a bird's eye view; it's heavenly. This will be our spot.

Fly high, my little sparrow.
Come high above the care this world tries to offer you.

The view is bright and hopeful from Point Clear.

He shows her a whole new way of living. Love has perfect vision and no expectations. The love found at Point Clear is unconditional and without judgment; it holds no record of wrongs.

Things that have gone unnoticed come into view, like how much we are alike.

Let's stand together overlooking The Bay of the Holy Spirit at Point Clear.

I give you my love lenses, and they can't see sin.

20

Home

I love adventures. At first, I wandered far from home until I found my home was a person in a kingdom within me.

The day I found home, I was never homeless again.

I find myself at home in the bosom of Jesus, cuddled up in his love. I am held and snuggled in the innermost place and being of God. Here, in the secret nook of paradise, I'm home.

At home, I become fully acquainted with my Father. We spend a lot of time together.

And the King-man, who had no place to lay his earthly head, finds an eternal home within me.

What makes my Father's house home is my place in it.

He always had a home; he was looking for a house to put it in.

21

Resplendent Sky

She has met the Artist in the skies, and he has painted his expression in her.

She acquaints herself with the Artist's perfection and revels in his other works.

She is so familiar with his works that she can see hints of his masterstrokes and patterns in everything.

She understands now that everything he does is to the advantage of another.

She looks for him when she is not with him. She admires his work up close in his other expressions.

She travels the world collecting objects of beauty and unique value.

Everything he does fascinates her. His beauty never grows old.

She savors the sunrise and dotes on the sunset.

22

Expect Love

He made her to expect his love. He has never
not loved her. Sealed by love as love's prisoner,
closed off from her foes and locked wholly into
him.

She's spontaneous in his irresistible love that
pushes back fear. His beauty and love chase her
every moment of her life.

She discovered her value resting in his arms;
Never a doubt, she is loved.

The thought of her transformation stirred her
emotions. She hoped she'd never get used to
the way she felt about him.

She is his soul mate. They share the same
thoughts and finish each other's sentences.

She is a lover of all things he created.
Wonderer of all she meets,
Chiefly at himself in her,
and him in others.

23

Seahorses

She speaks seahorse.

She was in the depths of the ocean, swimming, exploring, adventuring, and just being herself.

She learned from the man pushed overboard that she could breathe in the depths of the Fair One's love and ride the creatures of the deep sea to the shores of destiny.

Naturally, she pointed east since everything otherworldly came from there and swam that way. Then swimming and remembering genesis, she caught the eastern current. She could have fought; the current wasn't forceful or violent, but she couldn't help but yield to it, so she relaxed and rode.

Pretty soon, she happened on a school of young seahorses using their tails to stay together.

Come with us, they whinnied.
We remember you. You are our Beloved.

Am I? I don't recognize you. She understood them.

A little blue one with a fiery-orange mane swam to her eyes and looked.

Oh, it's not him, but they're identical!
She must know him, and it whinnied with delight.
Do you know our Beloved, they brayed?

Yes, I know him. But do I really look like him?
She doubted.

We cannot tell the difference, they answered.

And she smiled and whinnied back.

24

Memories of Hovering

I stand at the edge of the ocean to feed my heart with memories of hovering. I remember the Spirit hovering, brooding, over the deep mysteries in the very heart of God.

The ocean spray catches the light as if someone had thrown a billion diamonds into the air, and he caught each one and hung them in the night sky.

I've been in him since before light began. And I remember the matter vibrating and humming and taking shape at the sound of his voice.

The ocean shares its memories of love spoken in the beginning with me.

I have the lover of the hover at the center of my being. He shares with me the memories of the matter.

He has created me in his image, so wild, radiant, and fierce that no single world can contain me.

25

Bella Vita

It's a beautiful life. Spend your days in Bella Vita listening to the language of love on the shores of the Blue Mountains and Emerald Coast.

Creation cannot stop declaring his beauty. Can you hear him?

Enjoy me, daughter.
It would help if you enjoyed the life I have given you.
Delight your heart in Mine.

The beautiful life is to be present in the moment, releasing the glory of God Jesus redeemed for mankind.

> Be where you are
> Take it all in
> Every moment is sacred
> My private sanctuary
> Enjoy Me
> As I enjoy you.

26

Highborn

Good morning, Princess.

She is a highborn young lady. The king is her
Father, and a royal river runs through her veins.
The thought of his love leaves her eyes misty.

Her voice is a source of pleasure to the king.
He has time for her. She is sure of his love.

She is undoubtedly the king's daughter, a
princess of the Way.

She has been drawn out of deep waters and
raised as a daughter in the king's palace.

She is the heir of all things. Does this ever sink
in?

She has found herself in the unexpected love of
the wild and beauty of the king's domain.

No longer alive by personal performance, her
reward is the king's triumph.

She was born into royalty.

Kindness is a Man

Is the school of kindness taught by the unkind? Or is it learned from receiving a loving Father's kindness when we expect something more like judgment and punishment?

His loving kindness is not a reward for good behavior but a Man to be received.

I saw the kindness in his eyes and turned to be face to face with him.

I spent time with a Man of loving kindness and grew like my kind, Godkind.

What if the fruit is a Man to be ingested?

Up, up, up. The fruit grows in the air. I feast on throne room conversations and become sweet.

Can we spend time bonding with a gentle Man and become like him to our brothers?

His kindness draws all men to return to him.

28

Raucous Ravens

The ravens are causing a ruckus today. I'll hardly be able to carry their generous portions. Where the ravens gather, a door to a heavenly storehouse stands ajar.

My preciousness is grounds for my safety and provision.

Am I his favorite; I lack nothing and I have more than enough.

I have no needs; he fulfills them all.

He is fascinated with me and longs for me to have the best. Perfect love is stalking me and tending to my needs.

Just let me know when you need more money, Husband says.

My preciousness to him guarantees my provision. In addition, I enjoy the benefits of being the Lamb's wife. All of my possessions are a gift from him.

29

Magic of Memory

She remembers a time when she felt
disconnected.

She sat down on the floor while the music
played, closed her eyes, and opened her heart.

She felt the Trio circling, hovering, dancing,
and twirling in love's delight around her. They
entwined her in the circle of their love.

She had antennas sticking out her heart, soul,
and mind, looking for love and connection that
she had never found in earthly things.

They reached out, held the antenna's, twirled
and laughed and cried and circled her. Then,
she saw bright strands of colorful DNA
forming in their hands.

She cried because she felt deeply connected for
the first time. She belonged with them.

Wired and designed for entanglement with the
Father, Son, and Spirit. Nothing else would
ever provide her completion but their love.

And she remembered a memory, a flash, a return, an awakening to her origin, life, and love in them.

A new sensation overwhelmed her, confidence.

She remembered whence she came from, born above, sure of the Father's love.

30

Sight

She explores the same light that engulfs the Holy One.

One morning she was lying in bed, and she felt his presence draw near.

I am giving you sight, My darling.

Her whole body buzzed and fizzed. She felt every cell come alive. Every cell had an eye; he opened it, and she saw.

She sees his love in waves of light, sound, and energy. And she saw that she was held together by the sound of his voice. She felt light and love illuminating every cell in her being.

She was enlightened, and she glowed a little brighter. Her bones smiled and sang to the Man of Light who gave her sight.

And she loved him even more.

She lives in the light of his sight. He sheds light on the greatness of our Father.

31

Swan Dive

I swan dive into your endless ocean of
unthreatened love. It's as smooth as glass.

The secret family swims over to adore me.
Why do you love me so? I say.
We love what he loves, they reply.

And they marvel at love's image and likeness in
me.

Even the little fish swim up and nibble on my
flesh, hoping to get a bite.

I swim in the glassy sea mingled with fiery love.
I'm weightless in the ocean of his love. I smell
the sea, clouds, sunshine, air, and limitless
space.

I immerse in the ocean of his love in the
heavenly realm; it cleanses me.

I swim in a love bath of restored innocence and
redeemed likeness; no wrinkle or scar of sin's
violence remains.

32

The Hyacinth Girl

The hyacinths in the fields beside Living
Springs have cute little faces and speak. They
call him *Husband.* They're in the know; they're a
close bunch, and they like to whisper.

I was bathing there when I saw them. I smelled
their sweet notes and admired their beehivish
hairdos as they swooned over him.

Lovingkindness goes before him.
He's known for goodness and mercy.
Look at how he takes such care of us.
There is none like him.

I dress after she bath in life. The flowers want
me to carry them.

Pick me, Pick me, they cry.
Oh, let the bride pick me.

The anticipation of the wedding is building and
bursting at the seams. Creation awaits as the
bride awakens to love.

33

Singing Stars

The stars sing as I walk between them, piercing the darkness. I am learning how to live in both worlds; one is more real than the other.

Once you hear the singing stars in the upper heavens, you can listen in the earth heavens. I never stop longing for the upper world, or inner as it's known to some.

Swimming in the starry universe, I feel the stars kissing me and following me as I go. I swim in a river of light among the heavens.

Then I see him, my flame of fire, my Bright Star. We envelop in a swirl, holding, spinning, laughing, singing, loving, and belonging to each other.

I've got you; he sings like a lullaby.
If you must look back, you'll see I have always had you. You mean everything to Me.

He is the Radiant Morningstar and the Star of the Dawn who is always singing and holding me.

34

Look What Love Made

One morning in the space between dream and awake, I saw a hand reaching out of the darkness for me. Then the Trio appeared, the Three that are One, looking into the open hand with tears of love and wonder.

I looked to see what they marveled over. In the hollow of the hand was a fetus the size of a peanut; I knew it was me.

Before I was in my mother's womb or my father's loins, I was in his hand. The Three were shimmering and fusing in and out of each other, but each was distinct.

With watery eyes and trembling voices, they said, *Look what We have made. You are from Us and like Us. You are Godkind of our very being and image.*

They doted and danced over little, tiny me. Then the one called Spirit put his mouth to my translucent face, breathed the breath of life in me, and I began.

And they sang, *Look what love has made.*

The Little Book

I dreamt of a Man who cut up a black Bible into bite-sized cubes.

Hand me the little book, Lord.
Eat it entirely, he said.
And he fed me the little morsels.
Bitter in your belly, but sweet like honey.

So, I ate it, and the book grew and became a Man in me.

In him, I found a snow white page, a blank slate, a clean canvas. A place where nothing was, no ideas about who I was supposed to be, no rules about how I was to behave.

What if I am someone other than who I've been programmed and trained to be?

Did the Man-book want to write a story never heard before in my life?

Could I become something new?

Hinterland

Come to Hinterland. The land beyond
everything you can see with your eyes, where
every crooked thing has been made straight.

Convinced of its reality, I'm a mere sojourner
and pilgrim in a shadowland whose geography
could neither confine nor define my true
inheritance.

I shift beyond the material world, time, and
space. I fix my eyes on what is unseen.

Light and color flood before me as if I am
emerging from the darkest grave into a city of
pure gold. Everything transforms. I have
stepped from the world of everyday existence
into another, more real, immeasurably more
touchable, more believable place.

I did not regret the country I left behind; my
faith took me to the point of no return.

I am Abraham's offspring.

37

Emmanuel's Breath

While I was crying in his arms, he stood up for everything that tried to come against me.

I am content in his hold, entirely secure. He plucked me out of all my afflictions, held me to his chest, and I breathed Emmanuel's breath.

He keeps me with his heart. He knew me before I had a name.

I told him my fears, word by word, until words became unnecessary, and he still loved me.

He listens to me cry. My tears are liquid words; he reads them all, keeps them, and reads them again.

I am aware I'm precious to him. My preciousness is the grounds for his safekeeping. I'm certain he will not let me go.

And I breathe Emmanuel's breath as I lay my head on his heart.

The Skin Tents

I am a heavenly place. I am the most sacred shrine in the universe, even more, beautiful and intricate in detail than the Vatican.

The love of the ages has made me his permanent dwelling place. I am a skin tent, a tabernacle, a tent of meeting, the holy of holies.

The human body hosts the most intimate place of encounter.

His name has found a face in me. His language has found a voice to speak. His love has found a life to flow through, into the world.

Within me lives an eternal king and his kingdom that has my full attention and has captivates my gaze.

The incarnation has happened again in me. God and mankind united in one person.

Where I go, you go.
What you say, I say.

39

Mistral

Let's ride the thermals, taste the jet stream, and breathe the wind, says the wind-riding woman.

The wind wrapped around her like a warm hug of love and whispered *Abba* in every tongue.

She hears the mighty rushing wind coming from "up where". This celestial gale blows away personal preferences and pretenses.

She's a Mistral; she has the wind's view of everywhere. She is a windbringer. She walks into a room and creates a whirlwind.

She knows the words of the wind is the oldest language in the world.

Soon, I will blow my Spirit wind of sonship over all flesh, the wind whispers.

Are you ready for a ride? The wind speeds past her like wild horses, and she catches it and rides on its back.

She rides on the wind, no longer earthbound.

40

Bright Eyes

His love eternally enchants me; he's wooing me.

His bright eyes drew me in like a deep well that could transport me to a different place if I stared too long.

I looked at him, dazed by the unexpected wealth of his gold eyes. A flow of color like firelight runs beneath his burnished skin.

I lifted my face to him and let his bright eyes burn the rough edges off of my thoughts. It seemed like he brought a gentle breeze, which carried my edginess away and brought me much peace.

I turned and faced the redeeming light of the love of God in Christ Jesus. And I learned from him by looking at his ember-glowing eyes.

He has the answers to a thousand questions in his eyes. I found the brightness of his eyes and stared until I transformed.

41

Memory Sweep

My darling, I will wipe away every tear and heal every hurtful memory. My love will erase every destructive and deceptive mindset from your memory.

My little daughter, I make all things new. I'll turn the bitter into something sweet. When I saw the look in Adam's eye, I knew I would do anything to cover him so that he would not feel ashamed or fail.

I removed the guilt of the earth in a single day.

Now, she's forgotten her death in Adam. Her only memory is a new birth in the Living One's resurrection; nothing resembles her previous identity.

His love has swallowed her whole and erased every futile self-effort or memory of not being good enough.

He keeps no record of wrong.

She has no wrinkle or stain of sin's violence.

42

Age of Aquarius

It is the time of outpouring. The Eternal Man is pouring out living water on the earth.

A shower of grace is coming to a generation to speak lovingkindness in every language.

We've been born in a time when wisdom and revelation are falling like rain, and he's expanding our hearts with each new droplet.

Occupy your mind with this living water.

Whatever defined you before defines you no more.

She allowed the word to wash her mind. And her mind became a river of life that flowed out of his world.

She became weightless, a purposeful word returning to the waters above.

Love is reigning in her heart. She showers everyone she touches with the reign of his love.

43

The Breath Man

There is a man born from the very breath of God.

Like a poem, the word spoken by the breath is more than one thing at once, and everything is a metaphor, a symbol of the Breather and the life he gives.

You can't tell from where I've come.
You don't know where I am going.
I live under the governing wind;
Sometimes, it looks out of control.

I dance on the wind of his breath between two worlds. I breathe his breath, and all rules vanish.

Short on breath; heavy on rules.
Heavy on breath; short on rules.

The breath man says, *Blow where there are no verses to describe what has not happened yet.*

The breath man says, *This is that.*

44

Victor

His name is Victor. His kingdom has no evidence of Ophis. A thorough fumigation has taken place, leaving the sweet aroma of life instead of the stench of decay.

Her Father held her on his shoulders so she could see with no hindrance. A Man who looked like a Lamb slaughtered was alive. He danced and leaped through the streets in the most joyful procession she had ever seen.

It was undignified; some were angry at the scene, crossed their arms, and murmured their disapproval at the extravagant display of victory. Their faces contorted as if they smelled a stench.

Victor paraded his defeated foe as a public announcement of the end of works and self-effort. Then, he showcased his trophies of grace, the ones alive in the finished work of the cross.

Most spiritual warfare isn't warfare at all; it's arguing with a defeated devil. It is finished.

45

The Hills are Alive

The hills are alive with the sound of music.
With songs, they have sung for a thousand years.

The Man-lamb was drawn to the hills alone to hear the voice of his Father, he had heard before in another realm.

I go to the hills when my heart is lonely.
I know I will hear what I've heard before.

The hills have ears that listen to the lonely. The hills hold memories of what he has spoken.
Oh, hills, remind me of what he says and how his voice sounds.

I go to the hills to walk where he walked and breathe Christological air.

He leaves an iridescent trail, and I follow. We slip away together, high into the mountains, into the heavenly realm. I hear his voice and remember who I AM.

(The Sound of Music, The Hills Are Alive, by Richard Rogers and Oscar Hammerstein II.)

46

Crazy Over Me

He is a fire, nothing but a fire of love, crazy over what he has made.

Beautiful, beautiful, beautiful, is my beloved, he cries.

The secret of my life is that he has wrapped me into him.

My beauty profoundly affects him, drawing him to me like a flame.

He dotes on me. Ask the sand what he thinks.

I am born of timeless love between the Father, Son, and Spirit.

I am starting to believe I am very loved.

His love is swallowing me whole and erasing every futile self-effort or memory of not being good enough.

I'm learning to rest in this love with no conditions, only that I open up and receive it.

Beautiful Feet

She lays maps on the floor of her inner
chamber and walks barefoot among them.

Beautiful feet are roaming the world, carrying
love's wonder and restoring it from decay.

The world belongs to her, the land heir. She
recovers and restores the land with his agape.

She covers her feet with milk and honey and
walks among the nations dripping promises of
reconciliation.

She reminds the world of the unstoppable plan
of restoration his resurrection set in motion.

How beautiful are the feet of the Man who
came for me, defying every obstacle to reach
me with his love?

The world is a ready audience, and the appeal
of the Gospel is prevailing. The harvest is
evident everywhere and gaining ground.

48

Night Vision

I can see in the dark. That's a gift from my
Father. I can see through mountains. That's a
gift from him too.

I drink the light that is love. Love that holds no
record of wrong and light that knows no
darkness.

The light has overmastered the darkness, and
troubles are only shadows. To see in love is to
see in the light of his face. So ember-filled
Lamb's eyes light my journey through the night.

He lit the lamp in my understanding so that I
could recognize the features of his face and see
his likeness reflected in myself and others.

His eyes are the light of love by which I see.

The same God who bade light out of darkness
has kindled a light in my heart whose shining
has revealed the very features of Jesus in me.

Faith is learning how to see in the dark.

49

Poet of Immortality

She is a poet. The author of the ages is her Father, and she gets it honest. She belongs to the Poets of Immortality; imagineers, dreamers, oracles, signs, and wonders.

She has words of fire in her mouth. She wears her heart open and aflame. The rhema of God ignites her; she writes from the inkwell of his heart.

He has given her an ocean of meaning in a drop of language. She knows the nutritional value of words. There's zero nourishment in conversations and writings regarding old performance-based mindsets.

She is a connoisseur of the language of love. As a result, she has a refined palette for delicious words that make his mercy tangible, testable, and tastable.

The alphabet of love worked its way into her soul, and she writes of an eternal life of love, and love of eternal life.

50

Persuading Blood

I hear the whispering of the blood; it speaks of better things.

A red river that carries love's conversation throughout the ages persuades me of mankind's innocence.

His blood inscribes a whole new language about original worth.

I believe in bloodlines. The Father took his time on mine.

I drink the blood of the vine. The blood entwines with my blood and bones convincing me of life and more life.

His blood becomes an underskin river, unleashing resurrection life within. I hear it speaking to me now, even as I write.

It speaks of better things, a better way of thinking, and a better way of living.

51

Notes That Make Scents

Scents are like notes in a perfume that carry layers of meaning and resonance.
I smelt, and I felt.

Notes in perfume release a melody that I can smell, a nose symphony. A stray scent may feel like a remembered taste of a long-forgotten experience.

Notes on the wind sing me a song of smells that remind me of home or a memory of a place I was before I had a skin tent. I leave my mind to relocate to heavenly places. I ride the scents straight to his eyes.

He smells like new life, the lingering after the fragrance of womb fluids - little currents of electricity shoot through my skin. Life, life, life.

My senses feel electrified, I notice everything, and nothing escapes my awareness. I inhale and take it all in.

Savoring takes time; I have eternity.

Trees

Looking at the tree, I see all her books, decades of leaves becoming pages through which fall, winter, spring, summer, drought and flood, darkness and light, never stop telling its stories. Always growing.

Dear tree, I see your blank pages.
How many storybooks are inside of you?

You tease me waving your green pages in the wind. But, if I sit under you, whose story will I write? And where will it have occurred?

How old is the oldest book?
Book, are you older than your tree?
In whose dust did you grow?

If matter holds memory, then what am I reading on these pages? What unwritten mysteries do these pages contain?

Tree, I will read thee and remember and write an ancient love story.

53

About Judgement

He
Keeps
No
Record
Of
Wrong.

He
Does
Not
Remember
Sin.

In
Jesus
God
Measured
Mankind
Innocent.

Once
And
For
All.

54

Eyes of Fire

I noticed the fire of light dancing in his eyes. His eyes channeled deep into my soul, beyond sound, burrowing through joint and marrow into the depths of my spirit.

When I felt his love pierce my soul, I knew he had healed me.

He has amber eyes that glisten with fire. He doesn't have a dark side. He is rich in love.

The fire in his eyes looked deep into me and exploded into a massive blaze of light and power that consumed the darkness eating away at my beloved identity. It burned every speck of disbelief and reclaimed my innocence and likeness.

The flame in his eyes reignited my memory of In-ness.

He's my flame, the fire from whom I now burn.

55

Lamb Light

The Little Lamb is the lamp of the world. In Jesus, God measured mankind as innocent.

Behold the Lamb of God who takes away the sins of the world.

The priest never inspected the worshipper bringing a sacrifice. He examined the lamb. He ensured its perfection and spotlessness.

Behold, the Little Lamb has been inspected and measured for us and found perfect. He stands in the middle of a vast throne. He appears to have been slaughtered but is now alive.

The Lamb is the lantern in my heart by which my path is alight. He shares his perfection with me.

I follow the Little Lamb's glowing footprints through the dark.

He lights my future, and he lights the face of my Father.

Kingdom of Love

In the kingdom, the only law is love.

This is her Father's realm, and now it belongs to her. He has bequeathed the kingdom unto her by heirship and promise, not through behavior.

We rule on thrones of agape love. Here, we celebrate the full consequences of being loved.

The kingdom of love is not some future place but a dimension of light and love that's here now. Love is ground zero for her. In the heart of his love is where she's taught, refreshed, illuminated, adored, approved, and transformed.

Evidence of wrong isn't valid or admissible in the courts of love; it does not exist.

The kingdom works on the heart level, not the mind. It's a place where your heart goes and where God rules. To walk into the kingdom realm, you step past the skin of this world and into a new world.

It would feel like a hug if a hug were a place. And it's every imagination of heaven you've ever thought of, with more details, sensations, love, light, and life.

It's stranger still that the Father has filled this with things you've never seen or imagined, although it feels like your bones remember when you hear of it.

Do you believe in the mystical, the fantastical, the improbable, or the impossible? Do you think the things others dismiss as dreams and imagination exist? Do you believe in eternal life? Do you yearn for everlasting love?

The kingdom life is a realm of a different dimension, and it's above the horizon of the senses. In the kingdom, breath is life, words become human beings, Christ's body is bread, bread is sight, and love is nourishment.

She creates a safe space for others to open their hearts and enter the kingdom. It feels like a hug.

Antiphonal Songs

She sings songs she learned by listening to the grass grow. She sings in a strange language, words, and tunes woven into her from the winds and waves.

She traveled further into the memory of the beginning than she ever had in her life.

The power of his ancient song ignited her memory.

She was in him as he sang the stars into being, and the wheel of the stars began turning above her. She could feel his deep voice humming alive inside her chest.

And they sang antiphonal songs.

Creator bellowed, and creation responded before words and worlds.

He is the Maestro, the chief choir conductor drawing out the music within everyone that intertwines in harmony to reveal the full stature of divine inspiration (Francois du Toit).

58

Moments of Remembering

I knew thee first, he whispers.
I loved thee first.
B*efore you even had a name, I knew you.*

Before you were a speck in your earthly father's
eye or a dream in your mother's heart, you were
in God's thoughts.

Remember your water and Spirit birth, not
born in the flesh but from above in heaven's
heart.

All the moments of life are love's way of
bringing me back to the Father's heart.

Love knew me before God spoke any words.

*Remember your beginning before creation; you will know
you are from Me.*

The act of remembering is exceptionally potent.

59

Jebra

One day I went to the seashore to find the One in whom I see myself.

As I waited, I looked at the massive waves of the Atlantic. I heard the wind's whisper of affection, and he surrounded me like a warm, salty hug. I felt huge hands on my shoulders and saw two footprints behind me in the sand.

A sense of profound, settling peace spread from my shoulders to my entire body as I stood still, looking out at the foamy sea. I rested in the peace and enjoyed it with tears.

What is your name? I whispered.
Jebra, he said. *I am your terpsichorean. I am here to bring you into the dance of knowing. I'm on your side. May I have this dance?*

I reached out and took his outstretched hand.

We danced in invisible waves of light and sound that surrounded him. He held me, and I saw a timeline of my life where he had always held me.

60

Fear

It was the year of the Great Scourge of fear.

It felt like an invisible swarm of bees was chasing me and landing on my chest.

I've got you, his voice rumbled in me.

So, I stopped running and turned to face the fear.

His agape love dissolves the dominion of darkness.

The fire of his love shines light in every area of my heart and consumes me.

I give him my fears, and he owns them.

Now, I only have one fear left, it belongs to him, and I have none left over for any other.

Who told you to be afraid?
Can you remember the last time you felt scared?
Do you want to turn and face the fear?
His love dissolves the grip of fear.

61

Yellow Dress

The heiress of creation stepped out into the cool morning air and said, *Today, I'd like to wear a yellow dress,* and lifted her arms.

At the sound of her voice, a hundred little yellow canaries flew from everywhere and swooped in for a landing. They landed on her, causing quite a fuss. Then they flew away as fast as they had come.

She saw the little yellow feathers they'd woven into a beautiful yellow ballroom gown. She marveled.

She said, *I wish I had a bouquet of wild yellow roses to go with my dress.* And the roses heard her heart from afar and ran and jumped into her arms.

Later on, she spoke and harvested a whole crop of pecans.

This is her Father's kingdom, and he has bequeathed it unto her.

62

Exploring Love

She is an explorer. Exploring the vastness of his love is like a gasp that swells in your heart, tickles your nose, and moistens your eyes. It's a squeal with delight when finding another breadth of his love. Exploring becomes as easy as breathing, except most people, forget they are breathing.

He fills her life with the wonders of his love. The wonders discovered become stories to tell, testimonies of a life lived to the extravagant extent of agape love that beckons to other explorers.

She embarks on the inexhaustible adventure of knowing him, a perpetual journey of unending life and immutable love. The journey of bonding with the perfect Man, the Man alive inside, who shares his righteousness with her.

He reveals the secret of his crazed love for the world.

I want us together. I love you more than anything you could ever do wrong.

63

Like Heart

Spirit to Spirit, heart to heart, worship is two hearts alike. A heart yoked above to his heart.

Everything is worship to me.

Blinking eyes, my eyelids rise and fall at the wonder of the Man who became sin for me.

Breathing chest, rising, falling in adoration of the little Lamb on the throne, who was dead, yet is alive.

Worship is a frequency, a sound wave, and I ride into his eyes.

I am a mobile sanctuary, a house of worship, a living ark of covenant love.

I live to worship him, and I'm just getting started.

Anticipate Beauty

I anticipate beauty and value in every soul. I see what is exquisite and miraculous in people.

Thinking of beauty brings revelation into reality.

Beauty is a powerful magnet.

He is immeasurably beautiful and infinitely kind.

He's obsessed with me and wishes to find my company. So we sit together and stare into one another's eyes, and we reflect each other's wild beauty as in a mirror.

I've stared at his face long enough to see him in others.

And he smiles and says,
I am much more beautiful in persons.

The house is immeasurably beautiful and infinitely kind (Susanna Clark).

Searcher of Wanderers

He is the Searcher of Wanderers, although he
knows where they are. Nothing is truly lost; it's
only hidden for a time.

He recovers the wonder in the wanderlings.

The Darlings may leave Wonderland for a
moment in his story, but they'll always come
home.

He's the Father on the porch awaiting his
child's return and the Shepherd holding his
little lamb.

The reward of the Searcher of Wanderers is the
warmth of wanderlings he wraps around his
neck as he carries them upward. There's no
groveling required in the rescue of his love.

His eyes say it all,
I have found you.
You are safe now.
Let me hold you, kiss you, and carry you.
Don't ever leave me again.

66

Rapha River

Stay in the Rapha River until you shrivel up.
Get pruney. Let the voice of the river hide all
the other voices.

She has a river of healing flowing on the inside.

She is the river's daughter and strong as the
tides.

She tracked the river to its source and bathed in
the waters of life there.

Daughter, it is you I love, came the voice like
Rapha waters. The words themselves were alive
and dismantled castles built in the sands of her
soul.

Her expression rippled with wonder and joy at
what he had done in an instant. Light waves
rippled into her as the Son rippled the waters.

The healing waters led her.
The foodful waters fed her.
And she lived, truly lived.

Invincible Love

I am a bride in love.

I hang your locket around my neck and wear your ring on my finger. This love is invincible, facing danger, death, and things that scare me.

Passion laughs at the terrors of hell. The fire of love stops at nothing. It sweeps everything before it. Flood waters cannot drown this love. Torrents of rain cannot put it out. This love cannot be bought or sold.

I am a woman possessed by love's wonder. So, I'll live in the wonder of how I awaken jealous love.

My desires are union inspired. I abide, engulfed in his love. The fiery flame of his affection disintegrates everything that is not love.

As a bride, I place myself in the delicate care of my husband. This union of invincible love defines my life.

68

Woodsy Eyes

She sees beyond what is obvious.
She is not at the mercy of anyone's suspicious
scrutiny.

She sees the earth healed and the bride united.
She sees beauty in every soul.
She does not have woodsy eyes.

He took the judgment of all mankind and drew
it to himself.

She sees others according to the finished work
of Jesus.

She sees now. She washed the clay blindfold of
sin off her eyes in Siloam Springs, and he's
given her his sight.

She sees for miles. She looks beyond the
shadows people hide behind and sees hearts
longing to be loved.

She uses her heart eyes to see God's image in
mankind.

69

Favorite

She is indeed her Father's favorite. The focus of her Father's affection and attention. She believes in love's initiative to save the world and restore innocence.

Her preciousness to him is grounds for her safety and provision. He is her Father.

Born from him, she lives from love's deep acceptance. She is his very own.

Her heart is secure in his immutable love for her.

He whispers as he holds her close to his chest,
You are my favorite little daughter.
I cherish you.
If they don't want you, I do.

She's a wanted daughter, living free and unfettered from man's approval.

She lives in love's opinion of her and cannot hear other voices.

The Earth Responds

The earth responds to her. Creation is ready and waiting on her to grow up.

She's a shield of the earth. Creation recognizes her because she's like him.

He gave her the earth as a gift of love. This is her Father's world, and he has bequeathed it unto her.

When did we stop listening to the world he entrusted us?

So, she listens as the earth speaks.

She walks into the forest and says aloud,
I know who I am now, and you've been waiting. The restoration of all things unto him has begun. I am here to release you from your decay.

And the leaves on the trees begin to tremble and shimmer, and the forest claps its hands and responds.

71

Pain

Even her pain is his. He paid the price to be present in pain, so that they could be together in everything.

She cuddles up in his bosom, and he holds her close to his heart. His faithfulness sounds like a cello deep in her chest. She follows the sound deeper into him and finds a river of tears. He is a Man of sorrows, well acquainted with grief. He's not afraid of sadness or pain. He does not give her a verse and walk away. Rather than scolding her for being afraid, he holds her through the night.

His arms soothe her.
You are Mine, he says.
I've got you. I'm not in a hurry to fix you.
So stay here with Me, My love.
I've got you through the night.

In his arms, disappointment fades into new hope, and offense turns into understanding. Bitterness turns to the sweetness of forgiving.

Where there was pain, now there's a bloom.

72

Hothouse

Though the windows may be small and few, she is in the hothouse of his nurturing love.

Although white cinderblock surrounds her, she's safe in her Father's loving and affectionate arms.

The dirty past that led her here has now become the nurturing soil that enables her to grow and blossom in ways she would never have experienced on her own.

Under the fluorescent light, she found a gracious space to grow. Grace blankets every charge and takes the sting out. It covers and soothes her broken heart, and it's way out of proportion. Grace removed the weight off her shoulders and the chains binding her wrists.

His grace released her from every accusation and opinion that was not his, and she felt alive and free.

I see you growing, and I believe in you, My darling.

The Great Romance

There's no romance in the pursuit of riches or religion.
Both destroy the spontaneity that inspires and fuels a
lover's life (Francois du Toit).

She is living the most remarkable love story
ever told. It has layers of mystery, sacrifice, and
immeasurable love. It is a love so unreasonable
that you can only believe it exists in your heart.

Romance has become her religion, and loving
him makes her shine. Oh, how she shines.

You are My darling, he says.
I adore you, my King, my Spouse, she replies.
You are the love of all loves.

Dance with me, O lover of my soul
I hear the inward music
I can't help but move in tune with you.
Wrap your arms around me
Never let me go.

74

Clouds

One day she discovered alive in the One, a cloud filled with many others. (This cloud cannot be explained in earthly words.)

The Pharisees said, *Beware, you cannot speak to the dead. That's against the law.*

But the cloud dwellers are alive. They never die. They live to love the One and all who are in him.

She went to raise the dead but found a cloud instead. You can't raise someone who isn't dead.

The cloud riders encourage and cheer on the earthbound lovers.

Sometimes the cloud dwellers give us glimpses of glory or messages from the Father.

She's becoming a cloud alive; he's returning in her.

Face Aglow

While the rocks of her angry brothers rained down on her head, she glowed and forgave them.

She knows they don't mean what they say or do. She remembers that she, too, was once programmed and trained by religion to be afraid of freedom.

She is a living martyr. They couldn't see who she really was beyond their rules.

His love set her free and made her face shine.

Rivers of pain and persecution ignite fiery love inside her, and it spreads out of control.

Pain and persecution are the only accelerants in this fiery love, and she glows from the inside out.

The fire of his love has spread through every area of her heart and singed her beyond recognition.

Wonderful World

I see trees of green
Red roses too
I see them bloom
For me and you
And I think to myself
What a wonderful world

I see skies of blue
And clouds of white
The bright blessed day
The dark sacred night
And I think to myself
What a wonderful world

The colors of the rainbow
So pretty in the sky
Are also on the faces
Of people going by
I see friends shaking hands
Saying how do you do
They're really saying
I love you

I hear babies cry
I watch them grow

They'll learn much more
Than I'll ever know
And I think to myself,
What a wonderful world

And what a wonderful you.

(What a Wonderful World, Bob Thiele and George David Weiss.)

Here it Is

I lived, but I wasn't alive. So, I was on a ventilator of smoke and drugs for twenty-five of forty-two years.

I saw myself in a cold dungeon, lying flat on my back with no breath left.

When it was cold and dark, and I had been pronounced dead, he came to me and held me, and I lived.

Suddenly, a door opened, and a Man fully alive walked into the room and shone a radiant light.

He got up on the rugged stone tablet where I lay, and it seemed my back was against a door. He hovered, leaned down, and placed his warm arms under me. He put his forehead to my forehead, and he breathed. My eyes fluttered as he unleashed the breath of life in me.

Here it is. Arise, my Lambkin.

He carried me in his arms on high and placed me delicately in his Father's care.

The Lamb's Wife

She is the Lamb's wife. The priests inspected him in her place, and she was found pure and spotless.

She is serene as a little lamb in a sunny meadow.

She is mystically married to the Lamb. The two have now become One; no fear of separation in this love union.

Union is what his plan is about, and this mystical marriage gives her life meaning.

She floundered through life, looking for love in so many other faces until she saw him.

Her life unfolded in one look in his eyes as if their souls had been woven together before time.

He asked for her hand, and she reached out and took his name.

The Father's Fondness

She is the treasure he found in the field, and the Father is very fond of her.

She knows of his indulgence and obsession with her. He told her he thinks of her over and over again.

She has come to expect his affection and anticipates his love in every direction and every possible way.

Acquaint yourself fully with My fondness for you. Do not waste your time on anyone who does not believe you when you tell them how you feel.

Perfect peace is holding her. She never feels diminished in the Father's arms, and he hears her heart. He cherishes broken hearts.

She allows his fondness for her to manifest, and she reflects his wild love and beauty.

Never a doubt, she is his daughter and the center of his affection.

80

Blossoming

She is in a beautiful new season of blossoming.
Perfect love has sown his seeds of light within
her. She grows white as light.

He sings over her seeds, and they grow
instantly.

She has been kept safe from the harsh winter in
the greenhouse of his nurturing love. Secretly
she grows under the Gardener's keen attention.

Her soil is extraordinarily fertile. The divine
nature he planted within her grows and
blossoms right on time.

She is like a laborless lily, not toiling or
spinning, planted deep within the roots of love,
looking pretty.

The Gardener looks at her with tenderness and
says,

She's perfect.
She's just perfect.
She couldn't be any more perfect.

81

Bigger Inside

She has discovered that broken bread is the cure for blindness.

We are all born blind. Jesus broke the bread, and she ate. The bread became a Man alive inside her, and she beheld him.

He opened her eyes from the inside. She grew bigger on the inside than on the outside. Inside her is stored all the mysteries and riches of heaven in the Man-Lamb, fully alive within.

She is living inside out. She is Godkind with an appetite for more than what the senses could satisfy her.

His voice is food. She eats and drinks from a heavenly reality.

The world within her is greater than the world around her. Broken bread gave her sight to see a whole new world.

The Bread is alive, consuming her from the inside out. Who is consuming who?

82

Heiress

She is of royal blood. As an heiress, she no longer lives by the earthly realm of personal performance.

The Father rewarded her with the finished work of Jesus on the cross. His bloodline secures her position.

She was born to hold light, not darkness or cruelty. She is the daughter of the High One.

She lives on her inheritance and dines at the king's table. Royalty runs through her veins. He teaches her to rule with love.

She spends her days exploring the palace and the kingdom he has bequeathed. She bestows his kindness throughout the land.

The idea that she is not the expression of his image and likeness can no longer attach itself to her thoughts.

Never a doubt, she is the king's daughter.

83

Honey

Honey follows me. Even my pain has a honey tint.

Hug me in your honey today, Papa.

Milk and honey drip from his lips, and he bears no shadows in his eyes.

I cannot tell you of the sweetness of his voice. He is exquisitely tender and infinitely kind. There is no hint of judgment in his eyes.

Take me into your honeycomb, hive, and love nest.

I am your honey.

Take me to the promised land, where waterfalls of honey freely fall. Honey foams spill over the rocks, and milk rivers flow through the promised land.

Honey found me.

84

Lover

She has become a lover. She no longer reminds herself to love. Instead, she yields to her true nature.

He has expanded her heart.
Nearness will override principles.

Snuggle into Me, little lover, and you will not have to fix yourself.

He is the weaver, weaving her into a beautiful tapestry of love and knowing everything there is to know about her. He is working himself into her conduct. The leaven of love is rising in her.

His love has taken over. So now, she lives a lover's life, not toiling, spinning, or busy.

She knows the Father will do everything he wants to do.

His love fulfills her.

Love-giver, she whispers and nuzzles into him.

85

Baby Victoria

Grammy gave me my first baby doll, Victoria. I loved that baby with all my seven-year-old heart.

My motherly instincts knew to place my baby doll crib beside my bed just in case she turned into a real baby in the middle of the night. So I prayed Victoria would be real. It was childish, but I was untainted by disappointment. My parents never told me not to pray like that.

I was eight when my parents announced that my mom was pregnant. I was going to be a big sister. We laughed and cried and held each other with excitement.

On my ninth birthday, Joshua David Cannon was born. He was my birthday present, and a cordless curling iron, two answered prayers.

I had a real, live baby doll, and my heart knew that the Father had heard me. I fell in love with my baby brother, and the one who listened to my little heart. And every time I look at Josh, I remember the One who heard me.

Hidden Trail

She has found a hidden trail off the beaten path
- a pathway between worlds.

It's easy to miss if you go along with the crowd.
It's a lonely road at first.

She walked, and the whispers of the crowd
dripped off her like rain. She steps through
pools of gossip.

He came and sat in her darkness.

She sat down under a weeping willow. He
healed the wounds of broken promises within
her and breathed hope into every single
disappointment, even the ones she hid.

*I will comfort you in sadness, lift your head and
strengthen you when you are weak. I will laugh and cry,
abide and hold you. I will never let you go.
I bind myself to you, My love.*

So, she leaves everything she has to cling to
him. And she walks a little further off the
beaten path.

Private Ocean

She is born from above in the womb of love.

She realized her beginning in the womb of his love from above was way before her mother's womb.

She was in the hidden basket, the secret ocean of Spirit womb.

My mother's womb was my passport to planet earth. When I was womb bound, you burrowed through the thick cocoon of my mother's belly and glowed on me in my private ocean. In my darkened nest, his brightness shed light on me (Francois du Toit).

Into the waters of Spirit ocean womb, I go. Immersed in the waters of assurance, I began to trust.

I return again and again to the private ocean womb of the Spirit to remind myself who I AM.

88

Mahanaim Dancers

Come to Mahanaim, the place where the angels dance about Face. The place of returning. The children turn about to reface the Father from whom they came.

The angels dance in circles around the wanderers celebrating their arrival home. They dance of the love between two worlds. They came running to gather around her, staring at her and dancing.

And she laughed because she could see both worlds from whence she came. She has come home in so many ways.

She sings his praises. The One who she wrestled with, and she remembered his ageless eyes like a light that had pierced and opened her heart.

And the angels dance swelled, and she could hear them singing.

Whatever is born of God is destined to triumph over the world's system.

Weaving Words

She writes with the eloquence of God, weaving words with creative potential.

She speaks and writes in another quality and interfaces with the Father.

The words grow under her pen. They drop like a plumb line straight into her heart, and she recognizes it in her bones.

She has a way with words.

She takes ordinary words and gives them life and character.

She takes the mundane, and she breathes on it. She learned that from her Father.

She writes to invite others into his gaze and extends the reality of his embrace and endless love. Her words carry weighty men to a high place in an instant.

She writes of the life found in his eyes.

Honey Beach

Shipwrecked on Honey Beach.

Although the storm nearly killed her, she landed in her favorite place.

She met a man completely transformed by love. On tropical, sandy shores, they build a fire. He teaches her to use vipers for kindling.

He tells her the greatest mystery ever told. He's a dead man and alive at the same time. His life means nothing and everything.

Everything that happens now is kindling for the fire burning within her. The fire of the Man of Love is burning her, and nothing can quench this love.

Come away with Me to Honey Beach, where My love runs thick as the sand.
Cut away your earth anchors and leave them in the sea of forgiveness.
Co-crucified and now co-alive.

91

He is Not a Tyrant

He is kind.
He is not a tyrant.
He is not angry.
He does not raise his voice at her.
He has never yelled at her.

He is gentle.
He is tender.
He is safe.

His love lasts.
His love runs deep.

He is all goodness, all gentleness, all wisdom,
and all fatherhood.

He smells of sunshine and honey.
He is illustrious.

His eyes promise eternal love.
He is very fond of her.

He never turns away.
He always listens.
He holds her when she cries.

92

Sweet

At Meribah Springs, I drank, and strife turned sweet.

There is sweetness where there was once a bitter flavor. So I taste honey now, where I once tasted salt.

I drink and feel the sweet water branching through me. It's thick and sappy, like liquid love sinking deep into the marrow of my bones and soul.

Now filled with the sweetness of his soothing words, my mouth becomes a fountain of grace and inspiration.

I don't draw close to find something wrong with you.
My presence shouldn't make you feel like you are under investigation.
You delight Me.

Deep are the springs of his sweetness, deeper still in conflict. He unveils his ever-loving splendor in desolate lands.

93

Era

I dreamed of a young woman.
What is your name, I said.

I am Era, she replied.
She had a great laugh.

The era of laughter is the era of the freeborn.
The freeborn are children of promise, not of
self-effort.

I tried to talk to her. It was loud, and we were
rudely interrupted by an older woman. She sat
in a big comfy chair, tearing page after page out
of the law book and eating it. She was the one
born under the law. The lawyers mock the free.

I stood up and yelled,
Get out of my house. The law isn't welcome here.

No one stops the laughter of the freeborn.

The era of laughter is the era of the freeborn.
The promised child laughs.

The children of Sarah are free from the law.

94

Doorway of Light

It was the year I learned to fly. It was the middle of the night.

As I lay in my bed, I saw a golden door. So I got up, went, and knocked on the door.

A glowing Man opened the door, *Come in*, he said. The door flung wide open. The brilliant Man of white light with living flames around him spoke aloud and fiercely.

You are free now.
You are safe in the light of My love.
Come up a little higher.

The darkness dispelled, and the whispering ceased. The Man ravished my heart with his love.

Where there is love, it is never truly dark.

I'm in a safe place out of reach and no longer living under my circumstances.

I am taking flight.

95

The Tall One Smelled Me

On one occasion, while walking on golden streets, a group of Tall Ones approached me. They were gigantic, and I stood still, barely breathing, thinking they would pass me by and be on their way (probably to important kingdom business).

Instead, they came near me, and one leaned way down. I could feel his nose on top of my head. He inhaled through his nostrils, and I felt my hair get sucked straight up. Every hair on my body stood up.

Did he smell me? I thought.
Oh, she smells so good.
Smell her, he said to the others.

And they gathered around me and took turns smelling me and laughing. My smell intoxicated them.

The Tall Ones are fascinated with everything he has created, but especially with the very ones they keep watch over.

She Bloomed

She stopped to smell the roses, and she
bloomed and never went back.

Light, Light, Light,
And sparks everywhere.

The silence of the greenhouse feels charged
with expectation. Here is where extraordinary
things happen.

When it was still, she heard the rambling roses
adoring him.

She enjoys the fragrance of new life, savoring
the scent of every moment.

Blooming takes time.

Life electrified her senses, she noticed
everything, and nothing escaped her awareness.
She is accepted, enamored, and loved by the
Gardener. She is loved no matter what.

I love you more than anything you could ever do wrong.

Giver

His love language is to give me things that I do not deserve. He is a giver.

I have spent much time with him, his gift embeds in me.

He whispers,
Let me change your life.
I give you a life of adventure.
Life and more life.

He gives me things before my heart asks for them.

He has given me everything created. He has given me his very life.

He gives only that which is beautiful.

Each morning he gives me new mercies.
He has given me freedom.

You are free. You were a slave to religion. But, I have set you free by my great love.

Love Plan

For years she thought how they wanted her to believe until she sat face to face with him, and he held her. After that, she began to see him.

She came off the beaten path and out of the mainstream.

After she heard his voice for herself, she realized she had only been hearing other people's opinions of him.

She longed to know him for herself.
She spent time with him all alone.

Presence overrides rules; fundamentals and principles mean nothing here. The Father was like nothing they had taught her; he was far better than she dreamed.

In silence, she met I AM, and he took her to the beginning and showed her his love plan laid out over time.

In stillness, something extraordinary transpired. They became friends.

One Perfect Man

If the body of Christ were human, each person inside of him would be a tiny cell.

Imagine all these cells filling his body and working and living together in total harmony to create one perfect Man.

Each person carries a distinct role in the body and functions equally.

He is the head, and we are his body.

The cells in our bodies do not try to be cells. Instead, they are born knowing their function is to have a healthy body.

One day, we will be one perfectly functioning Man that never ages, tires, or gets sick and is seated above in heavenly places, enthroned on a throne of love.

100

The East Reach

The exalted Son sits at the Father's right hand, in the East Reach.

Rules change in his reach.
Rules change in the east.

He planted a garden in the east, a picture of a perfect man dwelling in an ideal land. His Son is seated in the East Reach, at the Father's right hand. A perfect Man in a heavenly land.

The Son of the east is continually rising with healing in his wings.

The three Potentates saw the star in the East Reach and followed it to the Christ-child. They came from the land of the Risen Son. Were they walking backward to the beginning? Did they come from another time? They had seen him from afar and longed to bring him their hearts and lay their lives at the feet of the Baby Savior.

The east brings the light of a new day as the Son shines on the faces of his dwelling places.

101

Popping Corks

I'm fizzing. A million tiny bubbles are dancing under my skin. I'm brimming with bubbles to the top of my head. I drank the living water from the Man-Lamb, and a thunderbolt of love struck a river inside me, deep in my soul.

Have you ever seen lightning strike a body of water?

The intensity of his burning and immutable love hit my heart. It broke open a hidden spring of eternal life within me, and love in preposterous proportions is satiating my soul.

The river within began boiling, burning with flames of love inside my heart. It bubbled and fizzed until I spoke an ancient tongue that he understood. The cork popped!

I have become a mobile river, a floating fountain, a sailing spring, a singing brook singing songs in the most ancient of all languages, love.

102

Upland

Although the feeling in Upland is familiar, it never gets old. Its soft, quiet air is such a relief and comfort to me.

I have become uninterested in the noisy bewildering world below.

It's peaceful up here.

This is where I belong.

I want to live where it is peaceful and full of wild things.

I was born here. I am learning to carry this world within me into other worlds.

I feast on throne room realities and stay co-seated in my beloved. I can hardly believe he's placed me here and that I get to love him.

He has lavished every blessing on me from the heavenly realm.

103

He Sings

She hears the melody of her Father's voice. He is the choirmaster, the conductor of songs. He glitters from afar and sings in the midst of his children.

He sings songs from another world. His voice is so pure and sweet that it melts her heart in astonishment.

She takes his voice and breathes it into a deep place within her bones, marrow, and soul where life began.

The singing king holds her close to his heart. He sings and watches her grow.

He is the source good.
He is the source of love.
He is always kind.
He is tender and gentle.

Love sings over her and kindles a fiery passion in her heart.

104

His Voice

I
Do
Not
Know
What helps
Me more
Than
Hearing

His Voice.

He
Holds
My Face
In
Nail scarred
Hands

And whispers.

Enjoy
My
Love.

105

Akroate

She's a good listener and listens intently. She listens to things grow and to nature. She listens to hear the heart of the matter.

She hears his name riding on the wind coming from Upland.

Acquainted with him, she hears his voice from above. What she heard distanced her from the effect of what she had suffered.

The listeners are more excited about listening to him than speaking.

She hears the song of people's hearts when they are talking. She listens for the fire within them.

Once, she was alone with the fire, and it spoke to her.

She listens to love, not to examine.

She listens and holds space for others.

Son of Man

His hair is like a cloud rippling white.

His eyes hint at visions and wonders trapped within warm fiery embers.

He wears a robe of righteousness covering all of mankind hidden within him.

A golden river encircles him as all things flow from him and return to him.

Pure honey drenches his feet.

His voice holds the voice of all humanity as he speaks on our behalf.

He could and often did go about his business unrecognized. A continual flow of power and freedom emerges from him, and peace layers out like ripples from his heart.

His arms create a grace embrace large enough for the entire world.

107

Unconditional Love

She lives a life of unconditional love that cannot be provoked or threatened.

She's learning to rest in love no matter what happens. She lives above circumstances, seated in the love lap above.

She's surrendered herself to the arms of love in his world. She brings his love into her world by being loved so deeply there.

She listens as he sings and hums over her an ancient love song.

She lives in love's opinion of her. He couldn't stop loving her if he tried. Love is his nature. He places her in his heart, and love runs deep in her blood.

You are the daughter of my delight.
You completely please me.
Take sides with Me against your self-evaluation.

Dare to live unconditionally loved.

108

Pierced Ears

She has been pierced in the ear of her heart by the revelation of righteousness.

One look at his beautiful, powerful face, and she felt her heart untangle as though it had been wound in a knot around itself for so long that she had stopped noticing.

Her heart had grown ears, and she heard his whisper.

Wonder spread its wings when she opened her heart.

She uses her heart to hear God's echo in mankind.

His righteousness pierced deep in her heart and made her completely whole.

You are perfectly and utterly whole by my righteousness. Therefore, I will never hold your sins against you.

Unimaginable Things

I learn unimaginable things when I sit in the Father's love lap. Wonder sweeps through me, curiosity and longing, and I see all the possibilities of love.

I begin to think as he thinks. It is beyond anything I've ever heard.

He speaks in tones and colors and breath and groans; I instinctively understand.

I marvel at his eyes; his beauty changes me.

I belong here in the bosom of the Father, cuddled in his embrace. His breath sounds like the tides rising and falling. He lulls me to sleep on his chest. I am at rest in his love.

He loves me so deeply that we need no words.

Maybe nothing I know from below will be left of me when I awake in his love.

110

Waywardness

She is not afraid of waywardness. On the contrary, she trusts the Way in everyone's journey to see the light.

He's got the whole world in his hands, and she trusts him.

She senses and knows the wanderer's eminent return. She has an inner certainty, a confidence that no one is unbegun. If he began it, then it is finished.

His kindness is running rampant through the pig pens and turning hearts home.

Can you hear the Father running out to meet his homecoming kids? Did you hear him ignore and interrupt the sinner's prayer with kisses?

My lost son is home.
I am investing all that I have in redeeming his original value.

Kisses override groveling.

111

Sognatore

She's a dreamer. She dreams deep. Dreams are messages from the deep heart of God.

She is learning the secret language of dreams.

She dreams of dreams that cannot come to pass without him.

The dreaming and creative parts are beginning to find their footing and run wild.

She is his love dream. She is his brilliant idea.

She dreams dreams from above, and she sees magic in ordinary things.

She inherits his dreams. She dreams in gold and emeralds, of thrones of love and a kingdom of life.

She likes to talk about things not quite of this world, something she sees out of the corner of her eyes, or something she has brought back over from dreams.

112

Religion

Religion is like chewing gum that has lost its flavor.

Religion is worse than drugs. I tried both and got addicted. Detoxing from drugs takes days. Detoxing from religion takes a lifetime.

As religion grew more complex, I broke free and flew away, searching for love and peace.

The labyrinth of religion causes you to forget your true origin in him. The deeper you go, the more it picks your beloved identity to pieces.

Now that the canopy of religion had been removed, I was free to grow in the direct sunlight and cool mountain air and fed from open skies with huge drops of rain and underground springs from the depths.

Grace intervened and set me free from a system of works and a treadmill of performance to know him face to face as my Father.

113

Starfish

She looked at the bright orange fallen leaf on
the rock in the riverbed and said,
It would be better if you were a starfish.

And it changed before her eyes and swam away.

Nothing is as it seems with our earthly eyes. So
may the Father fill your eyes with his beauty.

She radiates a conversation that flows from a
mind radically transformed by redemption
realities.

She has a different way of experiencing the
world and creation. Nature bends to the
Creator and his heirs.

Seas can be parted, winds can be calmed and
directed, harvests can be instant, and bright
orange leaves can become starfish.

114

Hold a Flame

So immersed in the burning layers of the divine,
the world has no hold on me.

I am ever burning upward in thought, feeling,
and endeavor.

I gaze deeply into his fiery eyes, and the fire
murmurs, whispering things I had long
forgotten.

I am not here to impress you with Me.
I am here to persuade you about you.
Your sonship is what I am all about.
Let my fierce love burn away any doubts that you are
not Mine.

And the fire in his eyes ignited my belief in him,
and I left everything to become a flame.

I am the fire's daughter, belonging exclusively
to love's eternal flame.

115

Whales

Whales are the limousines of destiny.

The running rebel, pushed overboard by angry brothers, was swallowed whole, and spat out on the shores of destiny.

The Father isn't afraid you'll miss your destiny. Ask the young dove in the stormy seas treading to keep his head above water.

In the kingdom, running rebels, storms, angry pushing hands, whales, seashores, and cities to be saved, all point to destiny.

A man of destiny lives by the Father's very personal protection.

Let the rebels run and storms come, let the angry brothers push us overboard, swallow us up whole and spit us out on the shores of our destiny, Lord.

Oh, little dove, where are you flying?

116

Love's Acceptance

Her heart settled securely, knowing all is well
and all shall be well.

Her flesh snuggly nests in his hope, and his
vibrant beauty has gotten inside her.

And he whispers as he holds her close to his
chest, *If they don't want you, I do.*

She lives from love's acceptance.

She lives in the light of his love, and love shines
from her bones.

She is love's daughter. She belongs exclusively
to love. Love insists on her presence, not
demanding her to come, only longing with love.

She sees with love's eyes; nothing matters when
he is near.

She articulates the love story of Jesus, not
wanting anyone to perish.

117

Mobile River

She is a mobile river, a floating fountain, a
sailing spring.

Her hair is like a white cloud; it rains every time
the wind blows.

She drank and became a downpour.
She drank and a river gushed within her.

She is a calm, refreshing presence.

She gave the perfumed waters of his love an
opportunity to rinse her mind.

She echoes his agape and innocence.
She is his soulmate, and they have the same
thoughts. They finish each other's sentences.

Her river is teeming with life, and she feeds
many.

She is living water to all who meet her. She
irrigates dry souls and helps fruit grow.

118

Wave of Words

A tidal wave of creativity is calling to me,
Come and ride the wave of words.

Go with the flow. Raise your sails and catch the
wind to a whole new world.

Come out a little further.
You are going to love what I have planned for us.
I'm so excited about your life, darling.

I feel confidence building inside of me and
warmth in my chest that no one can take away.

I knew the first time I met this Man-word that
my life would never be the same.

He handed me a book in a raindrop. And I held
the book close to my heart. It began to hum
and sparkle, then turned into a Man in my
hands.

His words began to flow through me like light
and air. The message is a Man. The Gospel is a
Man alive that lives and breathes.

119

Adrift

She is caught adrift in love's opinions of her.
Love has taught her to fly on high winds.

She flew to the highest of all heights, and she
lived there. She made her home in the lap of
the Lamb.

She articulates the exact drift of the Father's
thoughts.

She has drifted beyond polarity, lost interest in
the world's self-absorption, and checked out of
the limelight that seduces most.

I'm so proud of you, he says.
I know it was hard to get here, but you made it.
Live in My opinion of you.

She left the earthly bounds behind and flew
high on the winds of his love.

I wonder if she'll ever come back, they said.

120

Human Chladni Plate

Sitting on the sandy seaside, I feel like a human Chladni plate. Suddenly, at the sound of his voice, my skin tingles, and I feel like sand moving and reforming into something more original, life-like, and akin to him than ever before. I am transforming, metanoia-ing, taking on his very image and likeness.

At the sound of his voice, I change.

He leans in and puts his forehead to mine, and takes my face in his hands. Little Lamb, to little lamb, the Darling of heaven is holding his darling. And I feel his love going deep into my memories like wine.

Remember who you are, he whispers.
I will guard you and protect you and provide for you. I'll cover you and defend you. Enjoy My love, My darling. Enjoy our likeness. Enjoy our Oneness.

And everything fades away, the sand, the wind, the ocean, and where there were two, now there are four dancing, and then there is only One.

121

The Scent of the Man

She smelled notes of myrrh, frankincense, rose buds, and oak, and her eyes followed her nose until she saw him. She caught the scent of the Man in the doorway. He was wearing beautiful perfume.

He created a breeze, and it tasted of roses and honey.

From the door, a great shaft of light descended. Within the light, the Man stood facing her. He was perfectly still. He was gazing at her, smiling.

At the sight of him, she felt strong.

His beauty and scent are refreshing. It smells like the fragrance of newborn life and innocence.

She savored his scent. It reminded her of her childhood.

She swore for a moment that she could see time ripple around her, granting her glimpses of the past through new eyes.

122

Alphabet of Love

There is no thorny language in the ancient conversation that echoes God's voice. Instead, the conversation flows from union.

The alphabet of love embroidered in our hearts speaks life and healing. For years they taught her thorn language in judgment and accusations.

Suspicious of love and raised to speak thorn, true love came and reminded us of our native tongue.

At first, it seemed like a foreign language, but our instincts knew it to be our Father's voice.

She sits in love's wonder and goes beyond anything ever taught before.

As he holds her and loves her, she remembers the alphabet of love and begins to sing again.

Wonder sweeps through her as she sees all the possibilities of love.

123

Kalodidaskalos

She is irresistibly lovable and beautiful.

She radiates a conversation that flows from a mind radically transformed by redemption realities (Francois du Toit).

Her eyes and ears are doorways through which wonder flows ceaselessly.

He made her his home. Her eyes shine with innocence, full of hope and goodness.

She looks normal on the outside, but a king and his kingdom with magnificent glory abide within her.

She is an astonishing place.

She is a sign and a wonder. And she looks with anticipation to see his beauty alive inside others.

She looks for the twinkle of life in their eyes that hints at the kingdom of life within.

124

The Great Disenchantment

The Great Disenchantment is when we stop listening to and caring for the world the Father designed for us.

I have a different way of experiencing creation. I relate to it as something that interacts with me. So when I observe the world, it observes me back. We reflect one another.

Creation is constantly speaking, and I listen with wonder.

Nature bends to the Creator and the Creator's sons and daughters, his land heirs.

I hear the groaning of creation and remind it of what's to come. The restoration of all things unto him, has begun.

Land heir announcement: *I'm here. I know who I am and what to do to release you from decay and give you life again. I'm a resurrected daughter with new life in my breath. This is my Father's world, and he has given it to me to care for and to love.*

125

Garden Door

There is a door that looks like a Man in the garden.

The hands of the door are frayed and worn by the passage of saints.

She stepped through the Gardener's Gold and Rambling Rose and up to the door. Rivers of golden light swooped her up like a princess.

Mary.

His voice carried her into his arms.

Not too tight yet, he said.
I am going to My Father's.
She could hardly let him go. She was slipping through the door into another world.

Go, tell My boys
I am going to My Father
and their Father
and My God and their God.

And the Golden Door opened to the world.

126

Heart Books

In the night, he whispered to her heart, and it opened. Inside was a library filled with books and stories of his infinite, unimaginable love.

Some books explain everything but do not see anything. These were not those kind of books.

These books had hearts with eyes and ears. These books were alive and waiting to be opened at the right time.

Where did all these books come from, my love?

And he said, *Every time you say I love you, in the morning, in the noon, in the evening, and while you sleep, your heart entwines with Mine, and your words come alive, and I write another love story.*

In the middle of the night, he spoke to her heart and inspired her with his love.

She awoke to a new day dawning and wrote of a love she experienced in his eyes. She writes of the whispers of love spoken in the night season.

127

Migration of Dragonflies

Oh, life of my life. I never thought I'd see the migration of dragonflies.

If I had not slowed down and let go of all devices, I might have missed the rare occurrence.

I had just been in the habit of looking up only a few months and, to my surprise, had experienced such a wonderful new life.

Sitting out back with only the chirping sparrows and occasional angry blue jay, I looked up to see thousands of dragonflies flying north, Upland. They came from all around. I could see them for as far as my eye would reach. Some flew high over the tops of tall oaks, and others flew just over my head, all on purpose.

As if there was a sound only their little blue bodies could hear, and they instinctively knew where to fly and who was calling them.

The Creator had whistled, and they were flying home for the winter.

128

The Thrill of His Arms

I refresh myself by looking at him with wonder.
The thrill of living in his arms never diminishes.

Kingly, his smile; thoughts overrun with love
for me.

I witness his immense beauty and receive his
mercy.

He's overwhelmed me with kindness. I have an
inner certainty he'll finish what he began. His
touch in me is permanent.

Lovingkindness and tender mercy are his
trademarks. He is not rigid in principles but
flowing in loving understanding.

He gives me things I have not thought to ask
for or earn.

I lay my head on his shoulder, and all things
cease; I'm out of myself, leaving my cares
forgotten among the lilies.

His arms never grow cold.

Hide and Go Seek

Catch me if you can.

Sunset at the waterside, the little translucent crabs exited their labyrinth and waved and teased us.

Dig your little holes and your underground maze.

I am over here now, one waved.

They hide from us. Do they want us to find them?

She becomes a seaside she-king, searching for hidden glory.

They played hide and seek with the little she-king in the afterglow. She laughed and played their game as she fed the wild imagination in her heart. She sees the world as a giant playground, the ultimate game of hide and go seek.

She seeks him and finds him everywhere.

130

Standing in a Sunbeam

She was at Inlet Beach at the end of May. The sunlight on the sea at sunset became a red ladder burning into the Son, and she climbed it. She brightens at the sight of him and begins to glow. Her eyes start to sparkle with innocence again.

She looked otherworldly as the sun began to set, lining her in gold.

As the sun set, the moon began to glow. The moonlight became a pathway into the deep, and she stepped out until she was over her head and plunged into the depths of his love.

She peaked the highest mountains of the sea and dove into the abysmal waters of his fathomless love. Yet, all the while, she still shined the like Son.

Are you standing in a sunbeam and letting it warm your body or are you sitting in a physics class and trying to understand sunlight?

131

Interior Castle

I venture into the interior castle built on the wonder of his love. All that I've known before seems worthless here. The deeper into the castle I go, the less I understand.

Within me is an unseen, eternal realm that has my full attention and has captivated my gaze.

I found a book in the interior castle. I recognized a word from the book, a deep, sudden sound, that bit into my heart and clung there until it came alive.

The book keeps speaking to me, although I've read it in several different languages and opinions. It has hidden inner secrets that only open to love.

In the castle lives a king seated on a throne of lovingkindness and unspoken mysteries loom between his heart and mine.

The kingdom of heaven isn't our goal, it's our beginning. We've been co-seated with the king in his castle of love.

132

Freaking Out

She is not afraid of fear, but sometimes she forgets.

She snuggles deeply into her Father's love lap and tells him; *I'm freaking out right now.*

He pulls her into his bosom and closer to his heart than ever and whispers, *You are safe here. Your life matters to me. Come to me afraid and I will protect you.*

He covers her in his love. She lets her heart hang on him. She hears the husky murmur in the deep bosom of his chest, and she clings to him.

Her tears stopped soon, but she still held onto him. And her eyes suddenly flashed; he had shown her a new way of seeing things. He is healing her sight.

She intertwined in love's tapestry.

An overmastering love filled her and overpowered all her cares, and the fear passed.

133

Lose the Crowd

There is an audience of One awaiting you. Are you willing to lose the crowd, to come deeper into the One?

Away from success formulas and man-pleasing and going along with the crowd; away from what is popular and normal. Away from social media and the limelight. Away from the predictable flows and the life plan, away from the acceptance or the wisdom of this world.

Would you dare to live a lifestyle where nothing is in your hands but the one thing that counts?

Your choices, or maybe someone else's, brought you here, but you cannot deny that you are here.

Alone? Not hardly.

But away from the world, society, the familiar, your family, your friends, and the things you once depended on.

In this place, you begin to cleave to Da Da, and he becomes your source of life and joy. In this place, you don't even know what will happen.

But, if he's with you, it doesn't even matter anymore.

(Justin Paul Abraham, Company of Burning Hearts, Podcast Episode 1, The Unknown Path.)

134

Port Escondido

She set sail and took shelter from the storm in Port Escondido. There she remembered who she was before she had become herself.

She heard the legend of the woman who had escaped her captors and hid there. She crossed the shores of Zicatela Beach and entered the waves of wonder.

She saw a tree growing in the ocean. There was a house in the tree in the sea. In the tree, she traced her origin back to when the tree was born.

In the beginning, she was face to face with God before time, space, or words existed.

She was in the tree, and the tree was in her. In the house in the tree in the ocean lives a king in a kingdom.

She is a princess.

135

Taker of Humanity

Who is this Man, the Taker of Humanity?

Who holds all of mankind inside of himself and dies our death, descending into our hellish nightmare?

Who redeems our fallen minds and disoriented image in resurrection life?

Who is this Man, the Taker of Humanity?

Who redeems the innocence of all mankind?

Ascending, his hands full of humans, forever seated at the right hand of the Father.

Who is this Man who takes humanity captive and places us in Beloved arms?

Who is this Man who bequests a kingdom unto us, the undeserving?

(St. Augustine described Jesus as the Taker of Humanity.)

136

Murmuring Fire

Remember your life in Mine, the fire murmured, whispering things I had long forgotten.

He breathes his fiery breath into my marrow and changes the shape of my bones, and I enter the fire. I burn and become light.

He is reaching out to me. He never stops. His presence is like a dancing flame engulfing me.

I stand in the fire, and his mind flows into mine. He burns himself into my imagination. Life between the ears takes its toll unless the mind yields to the fiery flames of undaunted love. The fire of his passion changes my mind.

It's easier to understand the fire than to remember to become it and allow it to overtake you.

While others study fire, I became it.

Fire to fire, feeding each other, fueling one another, and loving each other to flames.

Three

Green grass grow, I will watch you.

I see through light eyes. No sun, no moon, no stars yet. Only light.

My face against the new dirt smells the life waiting to be born. The most fertile soil, never seen the sun or moon. Brand new. I hear a language sung older than any human voice. Older than dirt. It enraptures me.

My face against the dirt, waiting to see the breath take form. And then the breath sang, every plant, every seed, every fruit, each filled with multiplying power, began to sprout.

Where my knees and face felt dirt, now green grass cushions and holds me, and the smell of the first blade of grass fills my nostrils. I smell sweetness and life.

Fresh-cut grass always reminds me of the third day, refreshing my memories of new life. I was there in him at the beginning.

138

Man of Fire

They came running to gather around him and stare at him and listen.

They came for warmth and light.

They came and could not help but sing and dance in circles around the Man of fire.

His ageless, light eyes were fierce and burning.

You are safe here.
You can rest in My warmth.
I will heal you.
You will find your strength again.

The fire spoke so gently to me. The promise in his voice moved me.

His ember-filled eyes pierced my cold heart with a revelation of righteousness and held me as I trembled.

The Man of fire is holding and warming me from the inside out, healing and making me whole.

Kite and Key

Fly your kite in a storm, My darling. The key in your hand looks brighter in the storm. I've given you no ordinary key; it unlocks waves and currents of energetic love hidden in invisible fields. Look through the storm.

The storm holds secrets for those brave souls daring to risk it all to ride a lightning bolt.

Hidden in children's toys and hearts is something so simple that it will leave the scholars of the day speechless.

Let Me strike the fire of My love and awaken a long forgotten memory.

Love in preposterous currents, able to shock the unbeating heart to the rhythm of life. The lightning of love pierced my heart and left me stunned. A sudden flash of lightning can reduce to dust, everything earthly.

More kites, more keys, more storms, more childlike wonderers, more Richard Saunders', daring to ride the lightning to its source.

Immanent Grove

She found the Immanent Grove. The grove of
God within. The Love Grove the place where
God permanently pervades and sustains her.

It seems like a grove of trees when she first sees
it. It looks like nothing much, but it draws her
heart. When she walks in it, she feels its life.
The foliage is always green with golden light.
Even on dark days, the trees hold some
sunlight. And in the night, it's never quite as
dark under them. The magic is strong here.

She spends days here pondering a page or line,
a word or a look from him.

They walk hand in hand.

She learns by looking at him. She learns from
the silence, the eyes of the animals, the birds'
flight, the butterflies' dance, and the great slow
gestures of trees.

*(I found the Immanent Grove in The Earthsea Cycle by
Ursula le Guin.)*

141

Unshakable Trust

They delight in one another. Their pleasure together overrode all, for their love was strong, steadfast, and unshaken by time and chance.

With him, she felt such a well-being as if he were in some place wholly defended from evil and harm. And peace clung to her thoughts in his arms, and she took it as a gift.

The friendship between them was a settled thing. He gave her the gift that only a friend can provide, the proof of unshaken, unshakable trust.

She must enjoy the life he paid for her to live. True, it is a life of great privilege and friendship. But, the quality of her life is important to him.

In the quiet mornings, they sit together. She longs to hear something profound. His nearness gives her access to mysteries, and so he whispers to her deeply,

Make sure you are enjoying Me.

142

Wrought in God

Made in heaven; wrought in God.

Love's hands formed her into shape by imagination and artistry.

She is elaborately embellished and ornamented.

She was made carefree, molded, shaped, formed, and fashioned with delicate care in the hands of love's wonder.

He has woven his affection into her.

She knows she's the apple of his eye.
She is her Father's daughter.

That which is born of the Spirit is Spirit. She discovered her genesis before her natural conception.

By design, she is Spirit-compatible. Spirit is her origin, not her mother's womb.

This eternal conversation of belonging, embroidered in her inner conscious, was woven into her, not with words, but with love and meaning. It is more dynamic and permanent than flesh.

Beloved, that's her; not defined by anything earthly, gender, nationality, history, culture, or religion. Nothing external defines her.

Only an ancient love that brought her forth in love defines her.

She was made in heaven and wrought in the Father's bosom.

(Thoughts on I John and John 3:21 from Francois du Toit, The Mirror Study Bible.)

143

I Love You

What if the only words I ever write are *I love you*, over and over again, every day for the rest of my life? My *leitmotif*, my never-ending love song.

It is enough.

These words carry layers and depths of meanings in my heart.

Some days they are light with airy love, and others they are heavy with wonder and thanksgiving.

I spend my days discovering the magnitude of grace wrapped up in omnipotent love and my nights adoring him.

I write *I love you* in every language,
Te amo,
Je t'aime,
Ti voglio bene,
Wo ai ni,
S'agapo,
Ana behibak.
He knows them all.

Made in the USA
Columbia, SC
06 December 2022

72828388R00089